EXTREME WEATHER

Blizzards

by Kay Manolis

Consultant:
Mark Seeley, Ph.D.,
University of Minnesota Extension
Meteorologist and Climatologist,
Department of Soil, Water, and Climate,
St Paul, Minn.

BLASTOFF!
4
READERS

BELLWETHER MEDIA · MINNEAPOLIS, MN

Note to Librarians, Teachers, and Parents:

Blastoff! Readers are carefully developed by literacy experts and combine standards-based content with developmentally appropriate text.

Level 1 provides the most support through repetition of high-frequency words, light text, predictable sentence patterns, and strong visual support.

Level 2 offers early readers a bit more challenge through varied simple sentences, increased text load, and less repetition of high-frequency words.

Level 3 advances early-fluent readers toward fluency through increased text and concept load, less reliance on visuals, longer sentences, and more literary language.

Level 4 builds reading stamina by providing more text per page, increased use of punctuation, greater variation in sentence patterns, and increasingly challenging vocabulary.

Level 5 encourages children to move from "learning to read" to "reading to learn" by providing even more text, varied writing styles, and less familiar topics.

Whichever book is right for your reader, Blastoff! Readers are the perfect books to build confidence and encourage a love of reading that will last a lifetime!

This edition first published in 2016 by Bellwether Media, Inc.

No part of this publication may be reproduced in whole or in part without written permission of the publisher. For information regarding permission, write to Bellwether Media, Inc., Attention: Permissions Department, 6012 Blue Circle Dr., Minnetonka, MN 55343.

Library of Congress Cataloging-in-Publication Data
Manolis, Kay.
  Blizzards / by Kay Manolis.
    p. cm. – (Blastoff! readers: Extreme weather)
  Includes bibliographical references and index.
  Summary: "Simple text and full-color photographs introduce beginning readers to the characteristics of blizzards. Developed by literacy experts for students in kindergarten through third grade"—Provided by publisher.
  ISBN: 978-1-60014-183-6 (hardcover : alk. paper)
  ISBN: 978-1-62617-463-4 (paperback : alk. paper)
  1. Blizzards—Juvenile literature. I. Title.

QC926.37.M36 2008
551.55'5–dc22   2008015216

Contents

What Is a Blizzard?

Fast winds blow snow sideways through the air. The snow is so thick that it is hard to see the house across the street.

This is a blizzard. It is a dangerous storm that combines cold temperatures, fierce winds, and blowing snow.

Some people call any bad winter storm a blizzard. However, a true blizzard must have blowing snow thick enough to block your view of things 440 yards (402 meters) away. That is about the distance of four football fields.

A true blizzard must also have winds that blow at least 35 miles (56 kilometers) per hour. These conditions must last for 3 hours or more.

7

How Do Blizzards Form?

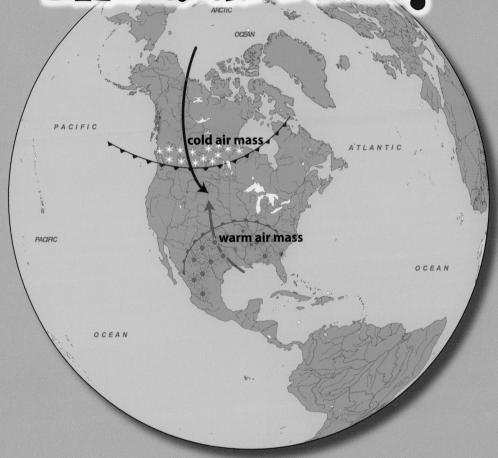

Blizzards bring wind. Wind starts when warm air meets cold air. Air is always moving over Earth's surface. The sun heats some areas of air more than others. A large area of air that is mostly the same temperature is called an **air mass**.

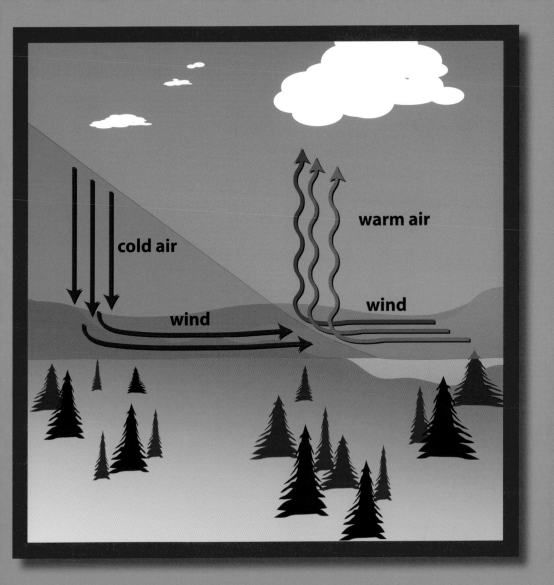

Sometimes a cold air mass and a warm
one meet. Warm air is lighter than cold
air. It rises over the cold air. The cold air
rushes into the space left behind by the
warm air. This makes wind.

In a blizzard, a very cold air mass meets a much warmer air mass. There is a big difference in their temperatures. This big temperature difference makes a blizzard wind very strong.

Blizzards blow snow through the air. They don't always bring new snow. Some blizzards blow snow that is already on the ground. This is called a **ground blizzard**.

fast fact

Antarctica gets very little snow each year, but it gets some of the world's worst blizzards. That means these are almost all ground blizzards. Because snow there does not melt, these blizzards can blow snow that has fallen over the course of years.

Some blizzards bring new snow. Warm air can hold a lot of **moisture**. Air cools as it rises. Cooler air cannot hold as much moisture as warmer air.

The moisture is squeezed out of the air like water squeezed out of a sponge. The moisture turns into **ice crystals** in very cold air. These can fall to the ground as snow.

fast fact

The Halloween Blizzard of 1991 dropped nearly 34 inches (94 centimeters) of snow on Duluth, Minnesota. It caused almost $70 million in property damage and knocked out power in parts of Minnesota, South Dakota, and Iowa.

In **severe** blizzards, blowing snow may make it impossible to see things right in front of you. You can see nothing but white. This is called a **whiteout**.

It is easy to get lost in a whiteout. People have gotten lost when they were just a few feet from their homes.

Blizzards make traveling hard and dangerous. They blow snow into **snowdrifts**. Snowdrifts can block doors and windows on buildings. They can block cars and even cover them up.

Blizzards are dangerous in other ways. They can knock down tree branches and power lines. Homes may lose electricity. Extremely cold temperatures can quickly freeze your skin if you are outside. This is called **frostbite**.

Predicting Blizzards

Meteorologists use satellites and **radar** to track winter weather. They announce a **winter storm watch** when conditions are right for a storm to form.

They put out a **blizzard warning** when they know that a blizzard is coming. People should stay indoors if possible during a blizzard warning, because it is dangerous to be outside.

"The Superstorm"

Blizzards can hit one small place or they can cover a huge area. One famous blizzard in 1993 covered most of the East Coast of the United States from Alabama to Georgia to Maine. People called it "The Superstorm."

There is a lot of work to do when a blizzard is over. Snowplows plow the roads. People shovel their driveways and dig out their cars. Everyone works together to help clear away the snow.

Glossary

air mass—a very large section of air that moves over the surface of the earth; the air in one air mass is mostly the same temperature.

blizzard warning—an announcement that a blizzard is coming

frostbite—a condition when skin and tissue are damaged because of cold temperatures

ground blizzard—a blizzard that blows snow that was already on the ground

ice crystals—tiny bits of frozen water; ice crystals clump together to make snowflakes.

meteorologists—scientists who study weather

moisture—small amounts of water; some moisture is in the form of a gas that floats in the air.

radar—a tool that uses radio waves to track weather conditions

severe—very dangerous

snowdrifts—snow piles that are formed by the wind

whiteout—an extreme condition when blowing snow makes it impossible to see close objects

winter storm watch—an announcement that conditions are right for a winter storm or a blizzard

To Learn More

AT THE LIBRARY

Erlbach, Louise. *Blizzards*. Chicago, Ill.: Children's Press, 1995.

Scheff, Duncan. *Blizzards*. Austin, Tex.: Steadwell, 2002.

Thomas, Rick. *Whiteout! A Book About Blizzards*. Minneapolis, Minn.: Picture Window, 2005.

ON THE WEB

Learning more about the blizzards is as easy as 1, 2, 3.

1. Go to www.factsurfer.com

2. Enter "blizzards" into search box.

3. Click the "Surf" button and you will see a list of related web sites.

With factsurfer.com, finding more information is just a click away.

Index

The images in this book are reproduced through the courtesy of: Getty Images, front cover, pp. 14, 16-17, 20-21; Jonathan Fickles / Getty Images, pp. 4-5; Dainis Derics, pp. 6-7; Linda Clavel, pp. 8, 9; George Peters, p. 10; Geoff Howe / Associated Press, p. 11; Ellen McKnight / Alamy, pp. 12-13; Jonathan Larsen, p. 15; National Geographic / Getty Images, p. 17 (inset); David R. Frazier Photolibrary, Inc. / Alamy, pp. 18-19.